Space Travel

Written by Sarah O'Neil

2

This is a space shuttle.
It takes astronauts into space.

When they are in space,
astronauts live in the space
shuttle.

The space shuttle can stay
in space for up to 30 days.

The space shuttle brings
astronauts back to Earth.

Very strong rockets push
the space shuttle into space.

The rockets drop off when
the space shuttle is in space.

In space, it is very cold,
and there is no air.

Astronauts need special suits
to stay alive when they leave
the space shuttle.

The space suits keep the
astronauts warm
and give them air.

Astronauts work in space.

They put machines into space and look after machines that are already in space.

The astronauts also do experiments to find out more about space.

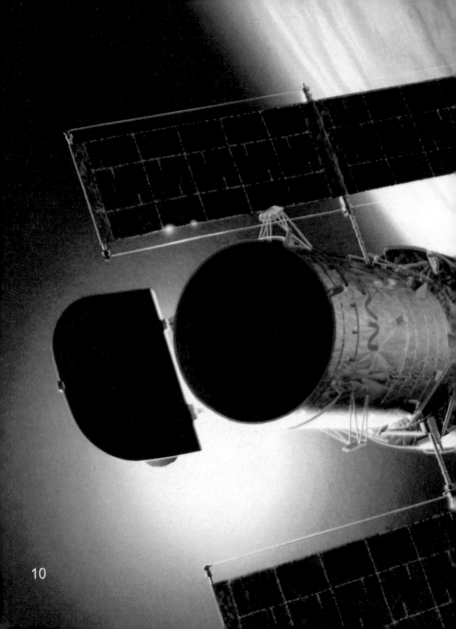

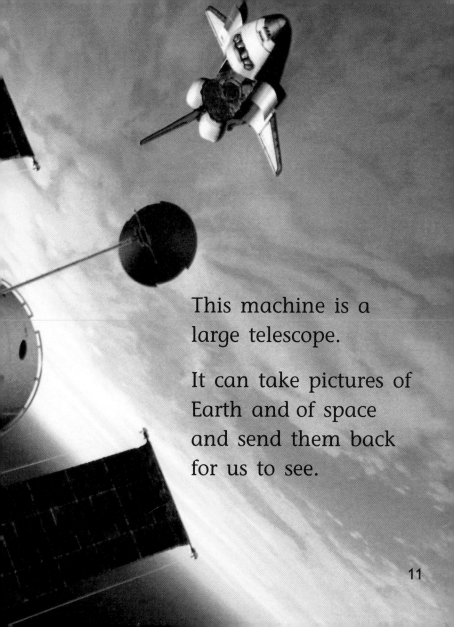

This machine is a
large telescope.

It can take pictures of
Earth and of space
and send them back
for us to see.

This is what Earth looks like from space.
The oceans look blue.
White clouds surround Earth.

This photograph shows mountains with snow on them. You can also see rivers and valleys.

Astronauts have landed on the moon.

The moon is made of rocks and dust.
There are many craters that look like
lumpy circles.

There are no plants or animals living
on the moon. The only water on the moon
is underground ice.

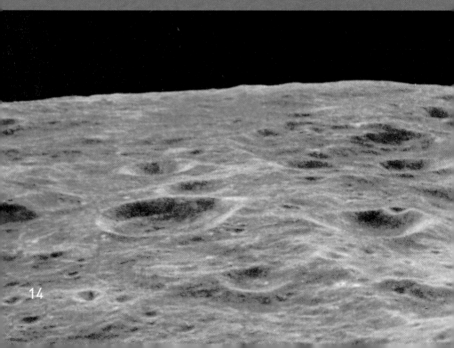

Someday, astronauts will go to Mars. The planet Mars is a very long way from Earth.